For my little hatchling, Emi.

First paperback edition published in 2024 by Flying Eye Books.

First published in 2020 by Flying Eye Books Ltd. 27 Westgate Street, London, E8 3RL.

Text and illustrations © Owen Davey 2020.

Owen Davey has asserted his right under the Copyright, Designs and Patents Act, 1988, to be identified as the Author and Illustrator of this Work.

Scientific consultant: Sarah Giltz, PhD

Every attempt has been made to ensure any statements written as fact have been checked to the best of our abilities. However, we are still human, thankfully, and occasionally little mistakes may crop up. Should you spot any errors, please email info@nobrow.net.

1 3 5 7 9 10 8 6 4 2

Published in the US by Flying Eye Books Ltd.
Printed in Poland on FSC® certified paper

ISBN: 978-1-83874-874-6
www.flyingeyebooks.com

OWEN DAVEY

OBSESSIVE ABOUT OCTOPUSES

FLYING EYE BOOKS

A Māori octopus
hanging out in a reef

CONTENTS

WHAT ARE OCTOPUSES?

Octopuses belong to the "cephalopod" animal family, which includes squid, cuttlefish, and nautiluses. Cephalopods are closely related to molluscs such as slugs and snails. They have soft bodies with little to no skeletons, large heads and muscular limbs, known as either arms or tentacles. Unlike other cephalopods, octopuses only have arms and almost always eight of them. In fact, their name comes from the ancient Greek for "eight-foot". Other cephalopods have a mixture of both arms and tentacles. Arms have suckers all along their underside, while tentacles only have suckers at the end.

Cuttlefish usually have eight arms and two tentacles.

Nautiluses have around 90 tentacles and live in a shell.

This common Sydney octopus has eight arms.

Squid usually have eight arms and two tentacles.

Home Sweet Home

There are approximately 300 species of octopus. They live in every ocean and are found everywhere from coral reefs, tide pools, seagrass beds, and kelp forests, to the open ocean and the deep sea—nearly three miles below the surface! The individuals of most species generally live alone, only coming together to produce offspring.

Nom Nom

All octopuses are carnivores, that means they only eat meat. They prey on a wide variety of sea creatures including fish, lobsters, clams, brittle stars, sharks, shrimp, sea snails, bristle worms, crabs, and sometimes smaller octopuses.

The varied diet of octopuses

Uncharted Waters

Through new technology we are learning more and more about these bizarre beings and the world they inhabit. Now we've had our many-armed introductions, let's chart a course to these curious cephalopods and get *Obsessive About Octopuses*!

BY DESIGN

Octopus species are split into two suborders: "incirrata" and "cirrata." Incirrata octopuses have no form of skeleton and can squeeze through tiny gaps only slightly larger than their eyeballs. Cirrata octopuses look slightly different, with shorter bodies, deep webbing, and fins above their eyes. They also have a small internal shell, which makes it harder for them to fit through small gaps. This coconut octopus is one species of the more abundant incirrata octopuses:

Mantle and Head

The mantle may look like a head, but it's better described as a body. It contains most of the octopus' vital organs including the gills, hearts, and reproductive glands, whereas the head contains the octopus' central brain, mouth, and eyes.

Eyes

Octopuses have large eyes that see well in both light and dark. It was once thought that they were color-blind, but they actually just see color in a different way to humans. They use their strangely shaped pupils to allow light into their eyes from many angles.

Cirrata octopuses are named after their "cirri," which are small hairlike strands similar to taste buds, found in pairs along their arms. Just like in this dumbo octopus:

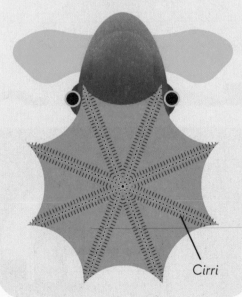

Cirri

Web

The arms are connected by skin, forming a structure called a "web." Some species have deep webbing, extending almost to the tips of the arms. The webbed structure can be expanded to aid with catching prey or swimming.

Mantle

Head

Arms

The majority of an octopus' nerve cells are found in its arms. Each arm can taste, touch, and move independently, without any direction from the brain.

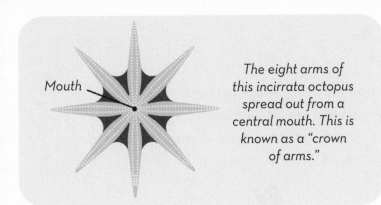

Mouth

The eight arms of this incirrata octopus spread out from a central mouth. This is known as a "crown of arms."

Suckers

Made up of an inner cup and an outer ring, suckers allow octopuses to attach to different surfaces, taste food, and handle objects and prey. When pressed against a surface, octopuses use their muscles to increase air pressure, creating a seal that is hard to break.

Siphon

This muscular funnel or tube is mainly used to expel water. The water is sucked into the mantle, over the gills through another opening, then pushed out of the siphon along with waste.

Siphon

Beak

Believe it or not, octopuses have beaks, similar to birds. The tip of the beak is usually pointed and the base is wider. When brought together, the sharp edges act as a cutting tool.

Radula

Beneath the beak sits the radula. This tonguelike organ is spiked, with multiple rows of teeth on it. It's used to bring food into their mouths through an action similar to licking.

Skin

Octopuses can absorb more than a third of the oxygen they need through their skin.

This diagram shows the beak and tongue-like radula of an octopus.

Hearts

Octopuses have three hearts, which are located in the mantle. Two can be found under each set of gills, while a third, known as the "systemic" heart, circulates blood around the body.

GET A MOVE ON

Ever wondered how something with eight legs gets around? It turns out octopuses have several solutions to this question. Each type of movement has its own advantages and disadvantages, so they choose a mode of transport based on their needs at the time. Octopuses regularly switch from one mode to another in quick succession.

At a Crawl

Many species of octopus live a "benthic" lifestyle, meaning they live on the seafloor. These individuals spend a lot of time crawling over rocks and sand, using their arms. Each arm in turn shortens, anchors to the ground, then stretches, pushing the octopus forward. This "walk" is time consuming, but relatively safe, as octopuses can hide beside rocks or duck under cover if a predator comes by.

Each arm takes its turn pushing the Atlantic white-spotted octopus forward.

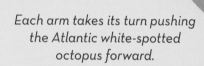

Walk on the Wild Side

Most animals have a pattern to their movement, known as a "gait." Humans, for example, move one leg, then the other, and repeat. This forms our walking pattern. Bizarrely, researchers have been unable to detect any pattern to how octopuses' arms will move at any one time while they walk—their gait seems to be a free-for-all.

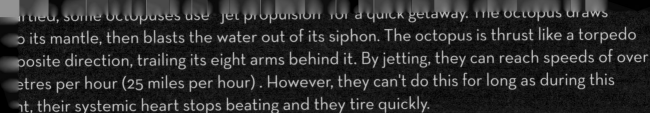

...rtled, some octopuses use "jet propulsion" for a quick getaway. The octopus draws
...o its mantle, then blasts the water out of its siphon. The octopus is thrust like a torpedo
...posite direction, trailing its eight arms behind it. By jetting, they can reach speeds of over
...etres per hour (25 miles per hour). However, they can't do this for long as during this
...nt, their systemic heart stops beating and they tire quickly.

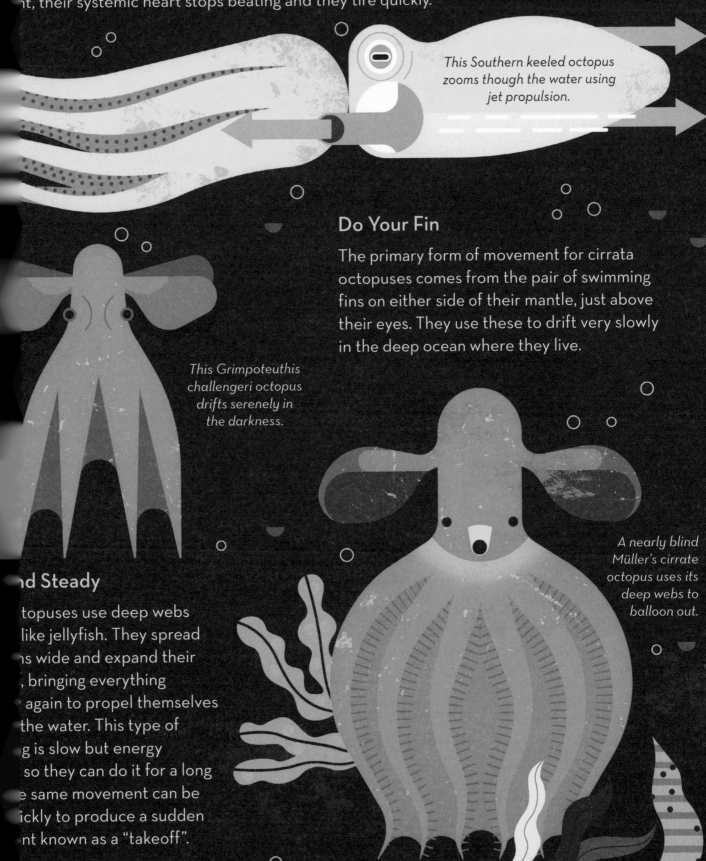

This Southern keeled octopus zooms though the water using jet propulsion.

Do Your Fin

The primary form of movement for cirrata octopuses comes from the pair of swimming fins on either side of their mantle, just above their eyes. They use these to drift very slowly in the deep ocean where they live.

This Grimpoteuthis challengeri octopus drifts serenely in the darkness.

A nearly blind Müller's cirrate octopus uses its deep webs to balloon out.

...nd Steady

...topuses use deep webs
...like jellyfish. They spread
...s wide and expand their
..., bringing everything
...again to propel themselves
...the water. This type of
...g is slow but energy
...so they can do it for a long
...e same movement can be
...ckly to produce a sudden
...nt known as a "takeoff".

DRESS FOR SUCCESS

Octopuses are masters of the costume change. They have the remarkable ability to change the pattern, color, and texture of their skin within a fraction of a second. Their brains control many thousands of different color cells called "chromatophores." These are found in their skin and are stretched, relaxed, tilted, or shifted to create different appearances.

Hide and Seek

Octopuses change the way they look to best resemble their backgrounds, making them hard to see. This "adaptive camouflage" is very useful for octopuses trying to stay hidden from prey or evade detection by predators.

One moment a day octopus looks like this . . .

. . . in a fraction of a second, it can look like this . . .

. . . or this. Blink and you'll miss it.

Rock 'n' Roll

Several octopus species are covered in fleshy lumps called "papillae," which can be extended to give them a spiky appearance, copying the texture of algae-covered rocks. These species masquerade as uninteresting objects so they are visible, but not detectable. This allows them to travel across exposed areas of sand by remaining in a rocklike form, moving at a pace that matches rippling light in the water.

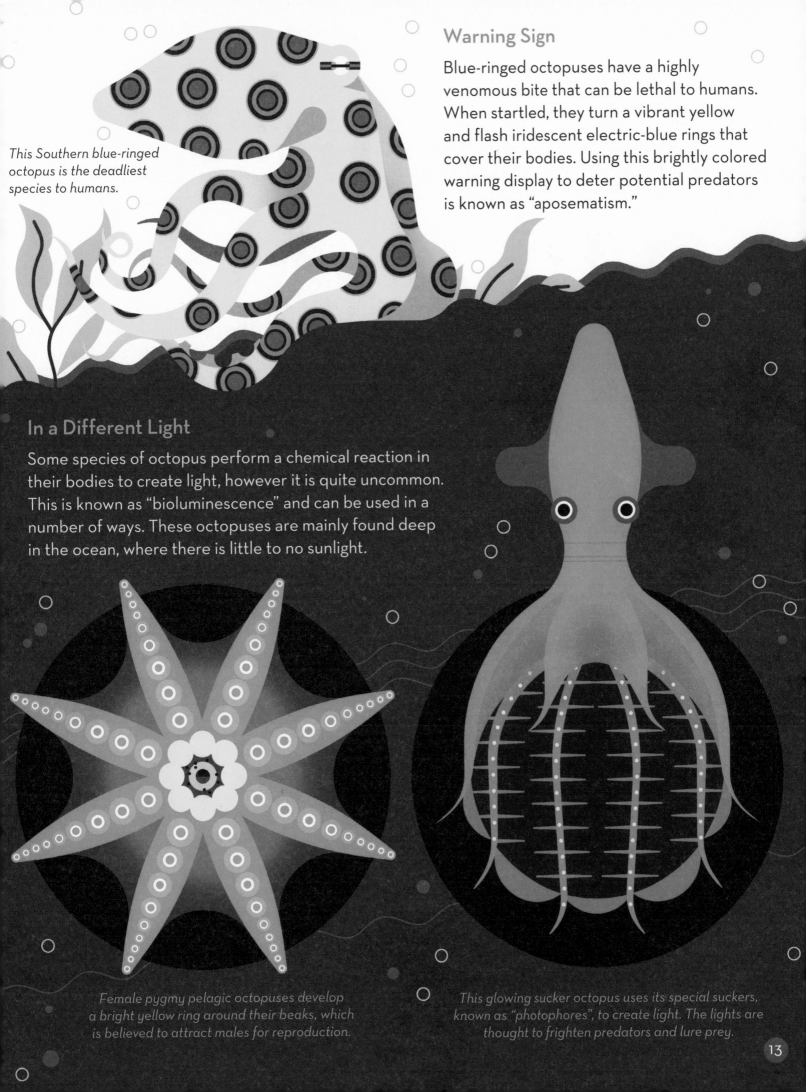

This Southern blue-ringed octopus is the deadliest species to humans.

Warning Sign

Blue-ringed octopuses have a highly venomous bite that can be lethal to humans. When startled, they turn a vibrant yellow and flash iridescent electric-blue rings that cover their bodies. Using this brightly colored warning display to deter potential predators is known as "aposematism."

In a Different Light

Some species of octopus perform a chemical reaction in their bodies to create light, however it is quite uncommon. This is known as "bioluminescence" and can be used in a number of ways. These octopuses are mainly found deep in the ocean, where there is little to no sunlight.

Female pygmy pelagic octopuses develop a bright yellow ring around their beaks, which is believed to attract males for reproduction.

This glowing sucker octopus uses its special suckers, known as "photophores", to create light. The lights are thought to frighten predators and lure prey.

ALL AN ACT

Featured Creatures: Mimic Octopus

Introducing to the stage, the one, the only, mimic octopus! This shape-shifting cephalopod is a true acting genius, able to mimic the color, shape, behavior, and movement of several different marine creatures. It is not yet known how many animals it can accurately impersonate, but it could be up to 15 separate species!

Role Call

Most creatures in the mimic octopus' repertoire are toxic, which is no coincidence. By pretending to be something dangerous or inedible, they are left alone. When an animal is protected by looking like an aposematic poisonous species, this is called "batesian mimicry."

No Small Parts

Mimic octopuses are also more than happy to blend into the background—sitting still and camouflaging themselves on the seafloor. Due to their talents at disguise, these octopuses can thrive in exposed sand habitats with little to no coral or rock formations, where other species would perish quickly.

Improv

The mimic octopus seems to choose its impersonation based on specific threats. When faced with a damselfish for example, the mimic octopus may act as a banded sea snake, a predator of the damselfish. Here are just a few of its starring roles:

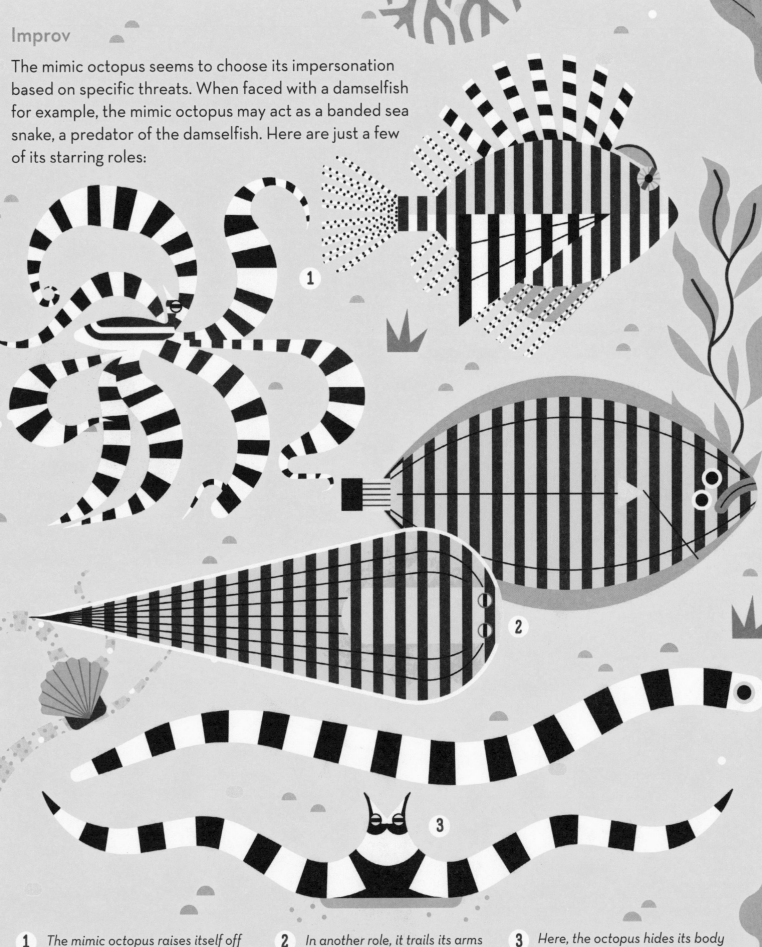

1 *The mimic octopus raises itself off the seabed and arranges its legs to look like the long spines of the venomous lion fish.*

2 *In another role, it trails its arms behind itself, swimming close to the seabed. Using jets, it performs a convincing imitation of the swimming motion of a fish like the banded sole.*

3 *Here, the octopus hides its body and six of its arms in the sand, then stretches out and waves the remaining two arms to impersonate a venomous sea snake.*

SELF-DEFENSE

The soft fleshy bodies of octopuses make them ideal prey for predators such as sharks and other large fish. Despite their sharp beaks and powerful arms, octopuses usually rely on staying hidden as their first line of defense. If spotted, however, they still have several cunning getaway tactics up their many sleeves.

Should I Stay or Should I Go?

When attacked, octopuses need to find ways to startle or confuse their attacker, scaring them off or giving themselves just enough time to escape. They have a few options to choose from to keep themselves safe from harm . . .

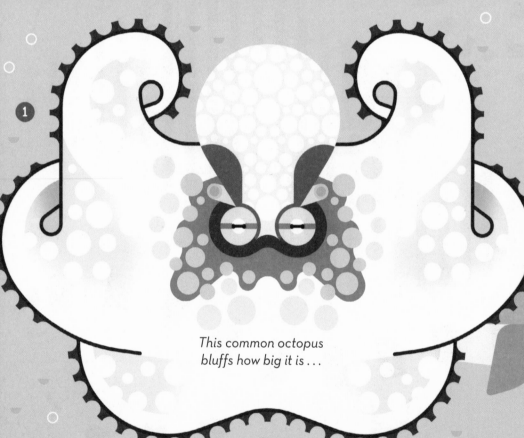

This common octopus bluffs how big it is . . .

. . . releases an arm . . .

1 Many octopus species spread out their arms, webs, or fins in an attempt to make themselves appear larger than they are. Some also produce dark rings around their eyes to further enhance the effect.

2 Some octopuses perform something called an "arm autonomy" when caught by a predator. Under stress, their arms can break off. The arm remains in the predator's grip, while its owner escapes. Octopuses can regrow these lost limbs at a later time.

The Home Advantage

Some octopuses construct homes from shells or create dens in caves and crevices, where they can barricade themselves in to stay safe. But these homes might not just be for escaping predators—some octopuses have been known to decorate their dens with shells, carcasses, and rocks. These "octopus gardens" may be used as an alarm bell for uninvited guests or simply to add a personal touch to their home, no one knows for sure.

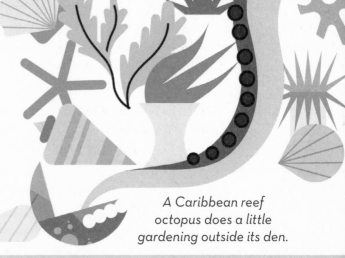

A Caribbean reef octopus does a little gardening outside its den.

. . . inks and jets away . . .

. . . and then camouflages against the seabed.

3 An octopus' ink sac is a handy tool for when a predator attacks. Located near the siphon, the ink is mixed with mucus and blasted out with water to create a black cloud in front of them. This ink provides cover for the octopus to escape, but also irritates the attacker and lowers its sense of smell.

4 Octopuses can use unpredictable moves to help them escape. This is called "protean behavior", named after the Greek god of unpredictability, Proteus. An octopus may pretend to go one way, then jet down to the seabed and camouflage itself. The attacker only has to lose sight of its prey for a second, and the octopus can seemingly vanish.

This hungry ornate octopus forages across different coral, using its arms to reach in and explore crevices in rocks to find food.

MAKING A MEAL OF THINGS

Octopuses are superb hunters and are able to blend in well with their surroundings to get close to prey without being discovered. Many will also hunt at night using their good eyesight to give them an added advantage in the dark. Benthic octopuses often explore large areas, clambering over the ocean floor in search of food.

Caught by Surprise

Octopuses regularly ambush prey by jet propelling quickly toward the creature, then dropping on top of it like a parachute, enveloping it with their arms and expanded webs. They will then reach under their bodies and use their arms to position the prey beneath their beaks. Sometimes the octopus simply grabs at the creature with its many arms, latches on with its suckers, and pulls the victim underneath it to its mouth.

Out of Their Shell

"Bivalves" are aquatic creatures whose bodies sit between hinged shells. Sometimes octopuses are strong enough to pry these shells apart and get to the fleshy body, but when a stubborn bivalve clamps itself shut too tightly, the octopus has another trick up its sleeves. It will bore a hole into the shell using its tonguelike radula, toxic saliva, and the "salivary papilla," which is an extendable saliva duct with miniature teeth. Once through, the bivalve's muscles relax and the shell comes apart.

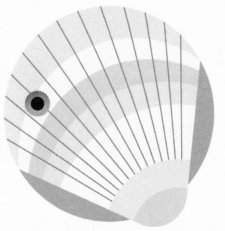

This clam shell shows the unmistakable bore hole from an octopus.

Piece by Piece

Octopuses paralyze their prey with a nerve toxin found in their saliva. They then use their beaks to bite chunks off their victim, swallowing the pieces whole. The process of eating a meal can take some time, so many octopuses prefer taking prey back to a den to eat in safety.

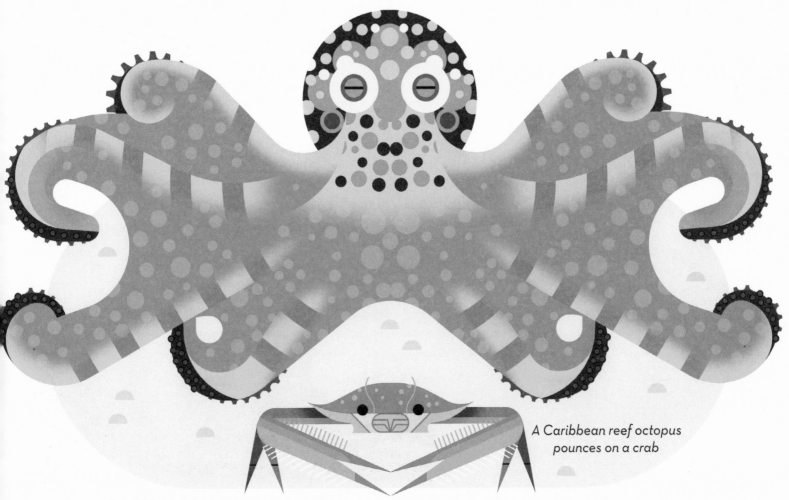

A Caribbean reef octopus pounces on a crab

Claws for Thought

There's no easy way to get through the hard shell of a crab, but octopuses have found a method that seems to work. Crabs are weakest at their joints, so octopuses often pull their legs off, then inject them with a paralyzing venom. This venom causes the crab's digestive enzymes to dissolve its own muscles, allowing the octopus to suck the crab meat out like a milkshake.

SMARTER THAN THE AVERAGE

Anything eaten by octopuses passes directly through their brains on the way to their stomachs. That's right—octopuses have donut-shaped brains! Despite this anatomical quirk, they are considered the most intelligent "invertebrates" (animals with no backbone) on Earth. Octopuses can learn by observing others, are able to recognize patterns, and have long- and short-term memory. This means they can solve puzzles and mazes, including working out how to unscrew childproof bottle caps!

Escape Artists

Octopuses are well known for causing chaos in aquariums. With the combination of their very flexible bodies and superb problem-solving skills, octopuses regularly wriggle free from seemingly secure tanks. Some octopuses have even learned to squirt water at light bulbs to short-circuit power supplies.

Oh no. He's escaped again!

This curled octopus is more than happy to collect an unlucky crab from a trap.

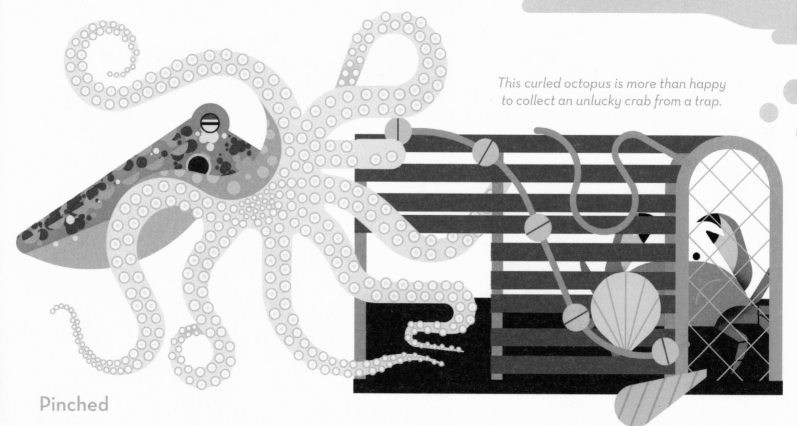

Pinched

Why go to the trouble of catching your own prey when humans can do it for you? Octopuses raid lobster pots to prey on trapped species, easily finding their way back out again when they're done. Some people even claim that octopuses have climbed aboard their fishing boats and "liberated" crabs from their stores.

Tool Up

The coconut octopus has developed the astounding ability to use tools. It collects coconut husks or shells and combines them as shelter to hide from prey or to protect themselves from predators. The truly astonishing part is that they have been known to carry this armor with them along the seafloor, ready to deploy it when needed. Gathering tools for future use requires an impressive form of intelligence and planning.

Move along please. No octopuses here. Just coconuts.

A Mind of Their Own

Some scientists believe that octopuses have individual personalities. Studies on ruby octopuses concluded that individuals fall into the categories of "passive," "aggressive," and "paranoid." Passive octopuses were generally quite shy, aggressive octopuses attacked anything that came near them, and paranoid octopuses would immediately ink and jet away at the slightest sign of trouble.

Do you think this ruby octopus is passive, aggressive, or paranoid?

Featured Creatures:
Star-Sucker Pygmy Octopus

The truly tiny star-sucker pygmy octopus measures in at only an inch (2.5 centimetres) and weighs less than a tenth of an ounce. It lives in the shallow waters of the western Pacific Ocean.

Life-size illustration of a star-sucker pygmy octopus

Featured Creatures: Giant Pacific Octopus

The largest species of octopus is believed to be the giant Pacific octopus. Their suckers can reach over two inches wide and each one can hold 35 pounds. Most adults are 10 to 16 feet long and weigh between 20 to 110 pounds. The largest recorded individual was a massive 600 pounds and had a 30-foot arm span. That's as long as a bus! They hunt at night, catching everything from clams, lobsters, and fish, to sharks and even birds.

Compare the size of this giant Pacific octopus with the diver next to it:

TO SCALE

Most octopuses are much smaller than the giant Pacific octopus. Here you can see the size of some other octopuses compared to an eight-inch pencil.

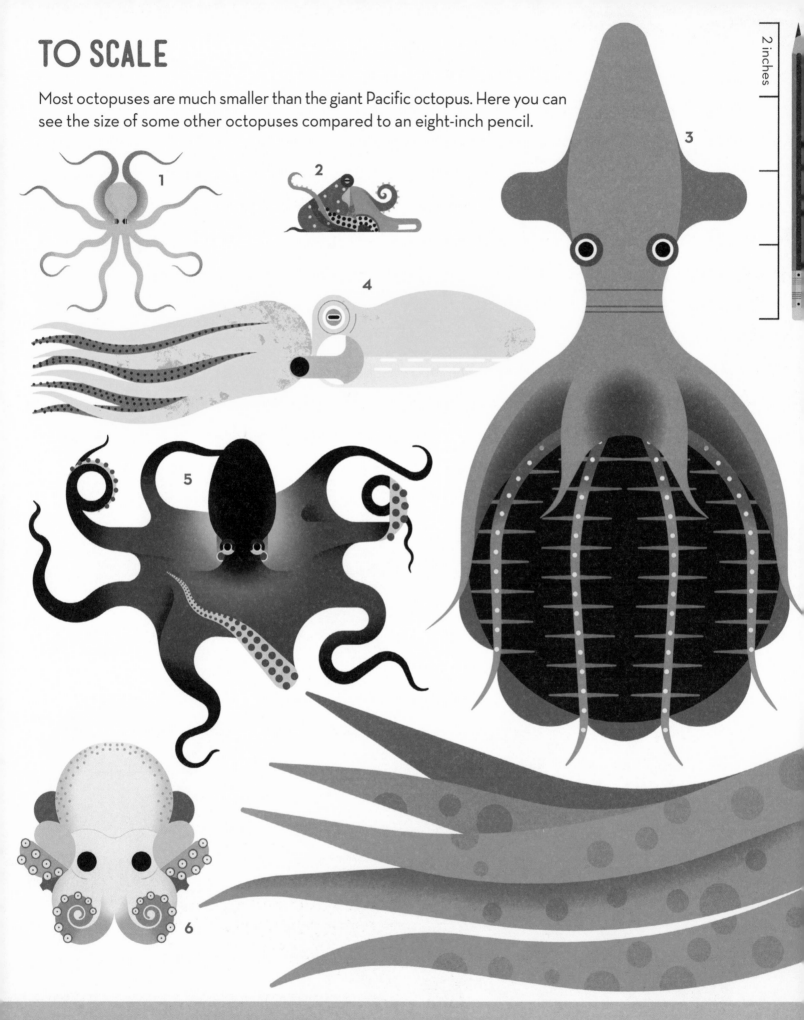

2 inches

1 *Webfoot octopus* 2 *Caribbean dwarf octopus* 3 *Glowing sucker octopus* 4 *Southern keeled octopus*
5 *Coconut octopus* 6 *Graneledone boreopacifica* 7 *Southern blue-ringed octopus* 8 *Ruby octopus*

9 *Southern sand octopus* 10 *Mimic octopus* 11 *Greater argonaut* 12 *Wunderpus octopus*
13 *Common octopus* 14 *Larger Pacific striped octopus* 15 *Algae octopus* 16 *Amphioctopus mototi*

BORN THIS WAY

Baby octopuses are called "hatchlings." This is for the simple reason that they hatch from eggs. Some octopuses can produce up to a million eggs at a time. Many species attach these to hard surfaces and guard them until they hatch. Other octopuses keep their eggs inside part of the reproductive organs or hold them in their mantle until the hatchlings emerge. Most octopuses are "semelparous" animals, which means they reproduce once and then they die.

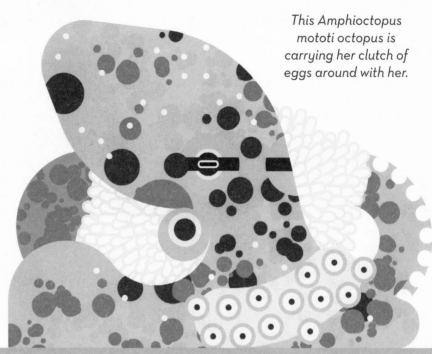

This Amphioctopus mototi octopus is carrying her clutch of eggs around with her.

A female Graneledone boreopacifica was recorded looking after her eggs for a record-breaking 53 months until they hatched. That's nearly four and a half years!

Baby Love

Octopuses sacrifice a lot to bring life into this world. Male octopuses have an arm called a "hectocotylus," which in some species is detached and given to the female for her to fertilize her eggs. Males also tend to die shortly after mating—and in some cases, they are even eaten by the female! It's not much better for the females either. Most female octopuses stop eating after producing hatchlings, and instead "brood," spending time blowing water over their eggs to keep them safe, clean, and the correct temperature. Once the eggs hatch, in many species the female's body begins to shut down and she dies shortly after.

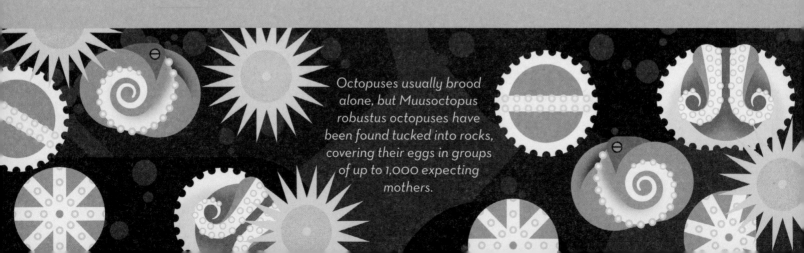

Octopuses usually brood alone, but Muusoctopus robustus octopuses have been found tucked into rocks, covering their eggs in groups of up to 1,000 expecting mothers.

All Your Eggs

Some octopus species carry their eggs with them in their arms or on structures they create, but none do it with quite as much style as argonauts (also known as paper nautiluses). Female argonauts secrete beautifully intricate paper-thin egg cases, where they store their tiny eggs. Females then live inside these "shells" with their heads and arms exposed. Unlike most octopuses, female argonauts do not die after brooding and can produce offspring several times in their lives. The males are very tiny in comparison to the females and do not produce shells. They only mate once before death.

The greater argonaut is the largest of the paper nautilus species with the most impressive egg case.

This Caribbean dwarf octopus hatchling hunts and catches an opossum shrimp.

Start Small

Hatchlings tend to grow to adult size in a short space of time. This is unsurprising, given that many octopuses live for just a few months—the longest-living species only reaching about 5 years old. Some hatchlings are large and look like miniature versions of their adult selves. These may take up a benthic lifestyle and begin hunting immediately or rise to the surface to hunt plankton. Others hatch as tiny "paralarvae," which are only around the size of a grain of rice. These become planktonic, which means they drift in the ocean's currents for several weeks, feeding on other plankton until their adult bodies develop.

Look how adorable these common octopus paralarvae are!

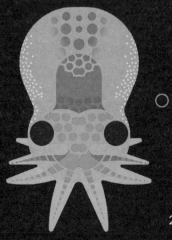

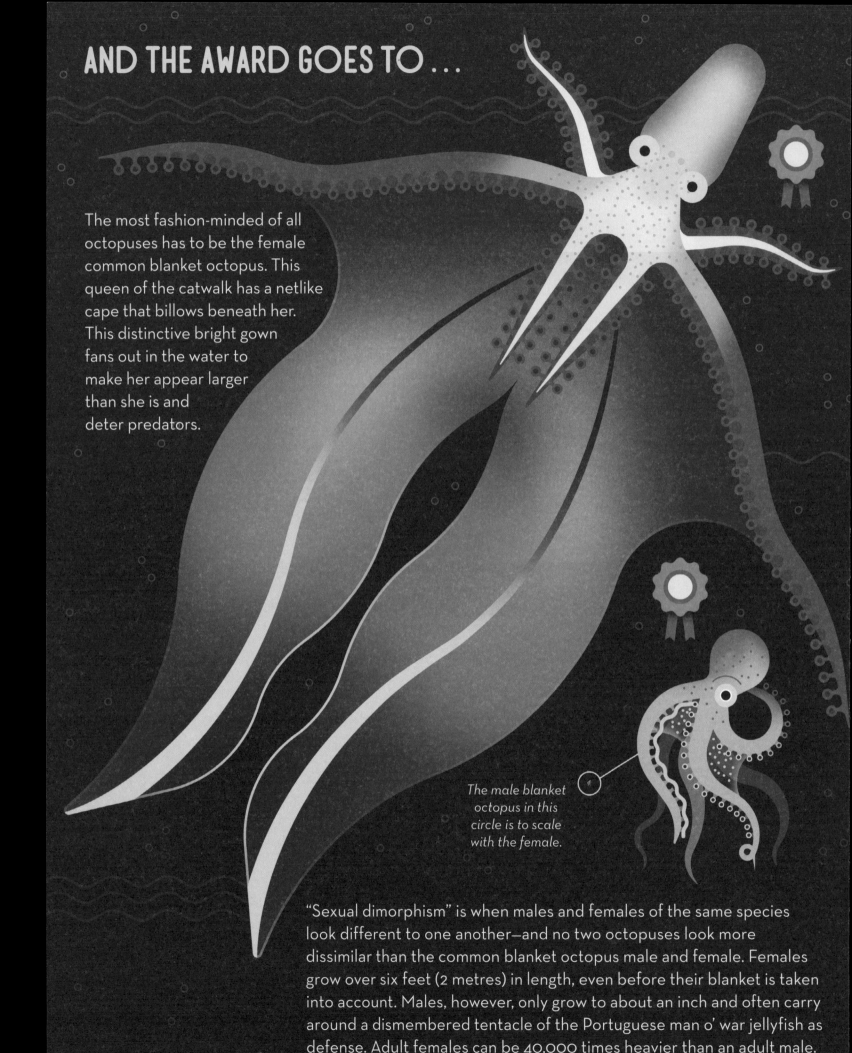

AND THE AWARD GOES TO ...

The most fashion-minded of all octopuses has to be the female common blanket octopus. This queen of the catwalk has a netlike cape that billows beneath her. This distinctive bright gown fans out in the water to make her appear larger than she is and deter predators.

The male blanket octopus in this circle is to scale with the female.

"Sexual dimorphism" is when males and females of the same species look different to one another—and no two octopuses look more dissimilar than the common blanket octopus male and female. Females grow over six feet (2 metres) in length, even before their blanket is taken into account. Males, however, only grow to about an inch and often carry around a dismembered tentacle of the Portuguese man o' war jellyfish as defense. Adult females can be 40,000 times heavier than an adult male.

Octopuses tend to enjoy their own company, living life alone, but larger Pacific striped octopuses win the award for being the most sociable. These octopuses live together in communities of up to 40 individuals. While mating, the male and female embrace, pressing their suckers together and touching beaks. Male and female pairs have even been discovered living and eating together.

The winner for best on land goes to the algae octopus. At low tides, these plucky predators hang out in tidal pools, searching for food. When one section of water is cleared, they push themselves onto rocks and go in search of the next pool. These octopuses can survive for several minutes on land if their skin remains wet from sea spray.

The Southern sand octopus wins the award for digging. It shoots jets of water below it, pushing sand out the way and burying itself in the seabed. The octopus then uses mucus to reinforce this hole, creating a fully formed burrow for itself.

WEIRD AND WONDERFUL

Angel Octopus
Angel octopuses have large eyes, a single line of suckers on each arm, and are covered in wartlike bumps.

Glass Octopus
Glass octopuses have almost completely transparent skin and bizarre, tubelike eyes.

California Two-Spot Octopus
The California two-spot octopus has distinctive bright eyespots called "ocelli" on its skin, which are only visible when the octopus is surprised or threatened.

Wunderpus Octopus

Unlike many octopuses, the pattern on a wunderpus octopus' skin is fixed and it has small eyes on stalks.

Flapjack Octopus

The adorable flapjack octopus has deep webbing and a more flattened appearance than most octopuses.

Seven-Arm Octopus

The massive seven-arm octopus gets its name from the male's apparent missing limb. Though in fact, its eighth arm— the "hectocotylus"—is looped in a sac beneath its right eye.

OCTOPUS MYTHOLOGY

Akkorokamui

According to the Japanese Ainu folktale, spirits cursed a man and sent a part-human, part-spider monster to destroy his village. After killing many people, the creature was turned into an octopus by the God of the Sea and thrown into the ocean. The bright red "Akkorokamui" grew and grew and began to swallow whales and ships. It was later poisoned by the God of the Sea but learned how to use this venom on prey.

Cecaelia Sea Witch

In Native American mythology, a man from a Raven tribe came across a woman from an Octopus tribe with eight braids of hair. The man pestered her until she became angry and her hair transformed into tentacles. This sea witch grabbed the man from the Raven tribe and drowned him in the encroaching sea. The next day the man returned from the dead, but he left the Octopus woman in peace.

Kupe and the Giant Wheke

Māori legend tells of a giant octopus belonging to a magic man named Muturangi, who began stealing all the fish from the nets of local fishermen. A warrior named Kupe vowed to stop the beast and ventured onto the water in his canoe. When the octopus ambushed the nets once more, Kupe attacked it and chased it through the water. Their epic battle continued for a long time over a great distance, until finally Kupe triumphed, splitting the octopus in two. The octopus' eyes formed rocks in the sea and its body became the hills of a valley.

Kraken

The legend of the Kraken tells of a truly enormous cephalopod that rises from the deep and attacks sailors at sea, dragging whole ships beneath the waves.

33

CONSERVATION

Octopuses rely on a healthy ocean for their survival, but human activity is harming Earth's waters. Through global warming, the temperatures of our seas are rising. Warmer waters accelerate an octopus' lifespan and can cause hatchlings to emerge too early to make use of essential food resources. It has also been proven that global warming has a direct impact on corals, with large areas of octopuses' habitats becoming "bleached" and eventually dying out.

Waste of Space

Household waste often ends up in the ocean and causes the deaths of thousands of marine animals every year. Huge artificial garbage "islands" have formed in several locations in our ocean. The largest is around 1.6 million square kilometres (620,000 square miles), which is twice the size of Texas or three times the size of France. Most of this is made up of plastic, with some calculations suggesting that there are 250 times more plastic pieces in this one "island" than there are humans in the world.

What Can We Do?

Here are some tips to reduce your plastic usage and other ways to help make a positive difference:

Always clean up your litter and put it in the garbage can. You could even help with a beach-clean event! This stops trash from being washed into the ocean and keeps our beaches beautiful.

Eating sustainable seafood helps make sure that your food has been caught in a way that won't negatively impact the ocean. Look for this symbol when food shopping.

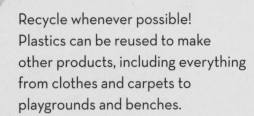

Avoid single-use plastic bottles by carrying a reusable bottle with you.

Did you know that most chewing gum is made of plastic? Ew! Try to avoid ones with "gum base" in the ingredients list.

Bring a reusable bag around with you so that you don't need a plastic one for your shopping. Try using a tote bag or something similar, there's thousands of designs out there.

Recycle whenever possible! Plastics can be reused to make other products, including everything from clothes and carpets to playgrounds and benches.

Say no when restaurants or take-outs offer you plastic straws and single-use cutlery. Try carrying reusable cutlery in your bag instead and if you prefer to use a straw, invest in a steel or bamboo one.

Walking, biking, and reducing how much electricity and heating you use can lower your carbon footprint. Carbon is absorbed by the ocean, but too much of it can make the water too acidic for marine life.

INDEX

ABOUT THE AUTHOR

Owen Davey is an award-winning Illustrator based in Worthing, UK. He has produced more than twenty books published in over twenty-five languages globally and often specializes in non fiction titles for kids. He also works commercially with clients including WWF, Google, National Geographic, and the BBC.

ALSO IN THE SERIES

"An absolute wonder . . . with just the right level of information for primary school kids to be truly fascinated and inspired to find out more. Highly recommended."

– BookTrust

"An all-round superior non fiction resource."

– Booklist

"An arresting and informative guide."

– Publishers Weekly